Feng Shui

A simple Feng Shui guide for beginners to use at home, the office, and at work for increased simplicity, productivity, happiness and wealth!

Table of Contents

Introduction 1
Chapter 1: Feng Shui 101: Basic Principles of Feng Shui......... 2
Chapter 2: Creating a Prosperous Home with Feng Shui........ 5
Chapter 3: Sloppy Office Atmosphere No More: Feng Shui to the Rescue 15
Chapter 4: How to Get Rid Of Negative Vibes with Feng Shui 19
Chapter 5: Feng Shui for a Harmonious Life: Love & Marriage 22
Chapter 6: 5 Feng Shui Tips to Remember For Good Health 24
Chapter 7: Feng Shui Colors 26
Chapter 8: Bagua Map 32
Chapter 9: Feng Shui Origins and History 42
Chapter 10: The Use of Nature in Your Home With Feng Shui 45
Conclusion 48

Introduction

I want to thank you and congratulate you for picking up this book; "Feng Shui".

This is the newly released, 2nd edition of this title. It has recently been updated with a range of new information, making this a complete guide to Feng Shui!

This book contains helpful information about Feng Shui, what it is and how you can use it. You will soon discover how Feng Shui has developed into the precise art form that it is today.

Feng Shui can have a huge impact on your energy levels, productivity, feelings, emotions, happiness, and success! The way things are placed in and around your home and office greatly affect all of these facets of your life.

This book will explain to you how to reorganize your home or office with Feng Shui techniques to transform it into a powerful and happy environment, full of positive energy, or 'Chi'.

You will discover tips and techniques that will allow you to begin successfully using feng shui in your home, office, or workplace, to increase the success and happiness you experience in all areas of your life!

This book will serve as the complete guide to implementing Feng Shui in your life. You will learn amazing ancient Chinese Feng Shui principles that you can begin implementing today!

Thanks again for taking the time to read this book, I hope you enjoy it!

Chapter 1:
Feng Shui 101: Basic Principles of Feng Shui

Do you ever feel like you have terrible luck? Or, maybe feel a bit uncomfortable in your surroundings? Does it seem like some negative energy is pulling you down? If you say yes to any of these questions, this book may be able to help you.

There are a lot of reasons why you might feel this way. It might be a bad day at work, an accident on the street or even a small incident that made you feel helpless. Take a deep breath and open your mind because you're about to learn one very important thing that could change your life – Feng Shui.

What is Feng Shui?

Feng Shui is a 3000 year-old art originating from China. It is a compilation of techniques for balancing elemental energy to ensure good health and fortune. The word 'Feng Shui' means wind (*feng*) and water (*shui*), two elements which are often associated with good luck, health and prosperity.

Now, you might wonder how inanimate objects can affect your life. How can Feng Shui even affect inanimate objects in the first place?

Feng Shui is primarily based on the Taoist ideology of nature, more importantly, the living energy all around the environment called *Chi* (energy). Under this vision, nature contains energy which must be balanced out to achieve the most favorable elemental conditions. Naturally, this includes arranging and combining elements in a specific order to balance both positive and negative *Chi*.

The art of Feng Shui also has its basis in the Chinese concept of *Yin* and *Yang* (good and evil). Because the Chinese believe that both *Yin* and *Yang* exist in everything, they developed Feng Shui as a way to balance out and counter the *Yang*. To do that, the Chinese had to figure out the elemental components of every matter in relation to space, location and direction. This is basically where the art of Feng Shui comes from.

There are 2 basic tools used in Feng Shui – the bagua and the compass.

The bagua serves as the energy map containing the symbols of an ancient oracle called *I Ching*. It is an octagonal shaped grid which will help you learn about Feng Shui areas in your place and how each area connects with specific points in your life.

The second tool is the compass, also known as *Luo-Pan*. The compass is composed of bands of concentric rings spread out around a magnetic needle. It is used to access more relevant information about a specific room or building. While the bagua figures out the ideal elemental compositions and areas, the compass figures its connection with space and direction.

The art of Feng Shui explores many aspects of nature such as colors and directions. It likewise uses several symbolic items like crystals, aquariums, clocks, fountains, figurines, rocks among others. A good Feng Shui expert knows how to put these ornaments together in order to create a positive Feng Shui for good health, relationships and fortune.

You also have to know that Feng Shui is not limited to one school of thought. This is why different Feng Shui experts will use different methods and symbolisms, so don't be surprised if you hear different views on Feng Shui. Despite such, all schools of thought revolve around the basic concepts of creating a harmonious environment – the balancing of nature's elements.

But Feng Shui is not all about an art of redesigning your furniture in your place. More importantly, Feng Shui is about re-aligning the *Chi* around you to what you are as a person. *Chi* is not limited to nature and your environment. You have *Chi* within yourself too! The greater challenge in the art of Feng Shui is not memorizing all the charts and symbols, but the process of putting it all together to work and take you wherever you want to go. Remember that everything contains energy, and the work of Feng Shui lies in making that energy flow within all things in a harmonious manner.

If properly done, Feng Shui can generally help you achieve success in life, business, emotional well-being and good health. Now let's get you started on your Feng Shui readings!

Chapter 2:
Creating a Prosperous Home with Feng Shui

If you're planning on doing Feng Shui, there is no better place to start with than your home. This is the place which has the most impact on your life, the place you stay most of the time. Doing Feng Shui in your home is like making an overhaul in about 50% of your life. Read on and learn more about making your home an ideal place to live in!

There are several factors that you need to look into when you are doing home Feng Shui and they are as follows:

- **Outside Feng Shui**

    The Feng Shui on the outside of your house is as important as its Feng Shui on the inside. The *Chi* flows around your place from outside elements which is why it's important to make sure you attract the positive energy to go in your home.

    Note that you'll be able to tell a good outside Feng Shui on the outset just by looking at it. Does your garage look okay to you? Does your surrounding make you feel safe and comfortable? If not, you can bet that you have a bad outside Feng Shui. Remember that the energy that surrounds your home affects your overall personality, more specifically your instincts. If your instinct is feeding you some negative vibes, be sure to listen to it and make a change.

    For starters, you need to clear out all unnecessary clutter. Clutter is a form of energy blocker which prevents your home from taking in as much positive energy as it could.

You should also try to avoid Sa Chi (attacking energy) and Si Chi (low and lifeless energy), or at least manage them. Sa Chi can be fed by sharp or pointing objects towards the main door. For this matter, try to avoid a T-junction house, pointed wall angles and sharp structures if you can. The farther these Sa Chi attractions are from you house, the less bad Feng Shui you attract.

Equally unproductive is the accumulation of Si Chi. Si Chi can be found in places where tragedy has happened. Avoid choosing locations where there have been tragedy, stress or death. Si Chi accumulates over time and it may stay in a particular area and this may affect your mood immensely causing you to feel as lifeless and depressed as the energy surrounding you.

- **Appliances and furniture**

Since Feng Shui is primarily anchored on nature and elements, a good home Feng Shui is expected to have lots of natural stuff. Electronic appliances are said to drain the energy of the home, so it must be balanced in three ways: by putting it in an area where its effects would be minimized, i.e. far end corner of the room, by cutting off its constant use and by balancing its draining effect through Feng Shui items, i.e. crystals and wood.

For instance, putting your television set on top of a wooden table would help balance the equation. You could also use some items to counter the energy draining effect such as putting on rice, salt and crystals as negative energy absorbers, near it. Despite the contemporary technology, try to put as much nature into your home as possible, such as wood, stones and water.

- **Light and ventilation**

    Good lighting and ventilation is a must for every home. It helps the *Chi* flow around your home easily, which is always a good thing when it comes to home Feng Shui. Remember that Feng Shui literally means 'wind and water'; therefore these two elements must take precedence over the rest. Having a well ventilated area takes care of the 'wind' essentials.

    To ensure that your home will have proper lighting and ventilation, put some windows in every area of your house. Note that while you can have fans and air conditioners, natural wind is still best in Feng Shui. Wind in its natural state contains more positive and free flowing energy than the stagnant/less rich air coming from air conditioning units.

- **Architectural design**

    Aesthetics and functionality need not be sacrificed in order to get a good home Feng Shui. While architectural designs take into consideration aesthetics and other practical things, Feng Shui helps put everything in harmonious order.

    However, to make the adjustments easier, it is best if you could incorporate Feng Shui from the very start of the project rather than later after it has already been finished. You would do well to hire an architect who has basic knowledge on Feng Shui or some advice from a

Feng Shui expert at the very least before constructing anything.

- **Energy flow**

    A good home Feng Shui ensures continuous and consistent flow of *Chi* all around the house. Aside from having good light and ventilation, your home must also have good *Chi* entry points, which is primarily through the doors.

    For this, the focus should be on your home's main entry. This is the point where your home absorbs the entire *Chi* that flows from the outside world. But what should you do to your home's main entry?

    For your home to have a strong main entry, it must be placed in a position where it can directly access the outside. It must not be hidden or blocked. It need not be a big door, just enough to accommodate as much energy flow as possible.

    Doors must also be positioned in such a way that the *Chi* does not immediately flow out without going through all the areas of the house. To be able to achieve that, avoid having parallel doors. Parallel doors allow the *Chi* to enter in one point and easily exit through the other. Instead, have the doors spaced out evenly. You could also use Feng Shui decors to welcome positive *Chi* in your home such as round tables, charms or even a vibrant rug.

6 Feng Shui Tips for a Good Home

Now that you have a good grasp of what a good home Feng Shui should be, it is now time for the execution. Here are some tips:

1. **Choose a good outside location**

   Because you know how important a good outside location would be for your home, make sure that you choose the perfect one. A good outside location is a place where nature is closest, and where Si Chi does not linger. For instance, do not buy a lot which is cheaper because it has been flooded or abandoned. The money you'll save will cost you in the long run. Choose a location which is vibrant and oozing with positive energy such as a good and quiet village in the city.

2. **Focus on the front door/ main entry**

   Your main entry will attract the *Chi* into your home. Make sure that you make it as attractive to positive energy as possible by putting Feng Shui decors and charms. You could also accentuate your main entry with some miniature water fountains which symbolize prosperity and success. You also have to eliminate energy blockers such as clutter. Most importantly, identify the bagua area of the main entry and let it guide you. After that, you should be able to know what you need to strengthen the flow of the *Chi* into your house. The bagua will help you identify which areas of the house are connected to specific areas in your life. For instance, if the main entry of your house is located in the Southeast portion, which is an area signifying wealth and prosperity, you'd be able to know what to put there i.e. wood and water elements.

3. **Establish good Feng Shui in the bedroom, kitchen and bathroom**

These are the most important areas in your home as far as Feng Shui is concerned. These areas are often referred to as the "Feng Shui Trinity" because they are the ones most connected to your well being. As a general rule, always make these areas lively and full of positive energy.

For good bedroom Feng Shui, take note of the following:

- A bedroom needs a relaxing and sensual energy. In order to create this kind of vibe, keep your bedroom as bare as possible. Get rid of the television set, exercise bike or stack of work papers. These things will remind you of work and responsibilities which can make it difficult for you to relax and sleep.

- Make the bed the focal point of your room and all other things just collateral.

- Maintain good air quality around the room by providing for good air ventilation or some air freshener/purifier.

- Do not put plants in your bedroom, no matter how small

- Have adequate lighting. Remember that light is one of the strongest Feng Shui sources of energy.

You can go with natural light during daytime or candles at night.

- The best Feng Shui colors for bedrooms are skin toned colors ranging from white to rich brown.

- Choose vibrant decor in your room that pictures what you want in life. Have uplifting artistic pieces rather than mystical, sad ones.

For good bathroom Feng Shui, take note of the following:

- Some have negative Feng Shui views when it comes to bathrooms because it is one of the areas where water, a powerful Feng Shui element, is drained out of the house. Do not be bound by this view. Feng Shui elements are supposed to go in and move out of the house, so there is really no problem there.

- The bathroom is a place where water is the abundant and dominant element. This might create an elemental imbalance which could result in bad Feng Shui. To cure this, you need to put some other elements such as Earth elements like small indoor plants or crystals. The Earth element is stronger than water, so even a small amount of Earth element can help balance things out.

- It is also good to have earthy tones in your bathroom such as gold and yellow for your walls or even for your towels.

- To balance out all elements, you can also pitch in some art decors in red (fire), brown (wood) and white (metal).

- Have some crystals hanging from the ceiling. As the *Chi* from the water goes down the drain, the crystals will help retain some of its energy so that the bathroom will not only be an exit point for the *Chi*.

For good kitchen Feng Shui, take note of the following:

- In the hierarchy of Feng Shui Trinity, some say that the kitchen ranks the highest, hence it's the most important part of the house. The kitchen also symbolizes wealth and prosperity.

- It is always a good Feng Shui to have your kitchen away from either the main or back door so as to let the *Chi* linger in this area longer.

- Keep the kitchen well-ventilated and clean at all times.

- Fresh flowers and fruits make for a good source of energy in the kitchen. Always keep a bowl of fresh fruits on your kitchen table. Putting some plants on your kitchen's window sill is also advisable.

- Yellow is a good Feng Shui color for the kitchen. You can choose between a variety of yellow shades i.e. squash yellow/ butter yellow or ginger yellow.

4. Choose the proper Feng Shui colors for each area of your home

In choosing Feng Shui colors for your home, it is necessary to first know the colors that represent each element.

- Water is represented by black and blue
- Metal is represented by white and gray
- Earth is represented by yellow, sandy and earthy tones
- Fire is represented by red, purple, orange and pink
- Wood is represented by brown and green

You need to know that choosing one color for all the areas of your house can be counterproductive. As you can see, the areas of your house should represent each element in the place where it should be strongest. Below are some color ideas that you may use:

- Green in the East Bagua Area to boost health and maintain happy family relationships
- Blue in the North Bagua Area to encourage career growth and wealth
- Yellow in the South Bagua Area for good, harmonious relationships and reunions
- White in the Western Bagua Area for heightened creativity and good ideas

Note that you need not color the entire area of your house blue or whatever color. Just make sure that these 'lucky' Feng Shui colors are dominant in the area specified. You can do this by simply adding a touch of colorful ornaments.

5. Determine your birth element

Your birth element connects you with the Feng Shui of your home. Remember that Feng Shui is all about making a particular arrangement work for you, and that means it will work only if it's in sync with what you are.

For example, if your birth element is fire, you should definitely put fire elements in your home such as red or triangular items. You would also want to nourish your element by putting Feng Shui decors made of wood as this feeds fire.

This will help you connect with the natural elements present in you and your home.

6. Go at your own pace

Lastly, you do not have to be pressured into doing Feng Shui all the way, especially if Feng Shui is quite new to you. Go at your own pace and determine the goals you want to achieve in your home. Only through this will you be able to really appreciate the power of Feng Shui in your home.

Chapter 3:
Sloppy Office Atmosphere No More: Feng Shui to the Rescue

The workplace is one of the places where people spend most of their time doing what they love to do. As such, it needs to be a place conducive to harmonious work relationship and productivity. If you feel like you are missing these things, Feng Shui might just be what you need.

Here are several Feng Shui tips that you could use to boost the energy around your workplace:

- **Clear out clutter in your work area**

    Almost every office space is filled with paper stacks, documents and other office supplies. The bad news? These clutters do not make work easier for you!

    Clutter represents old energy which can block the space for new and more productive energy to come in. By clearing out your office's clutter, you will be able to have the clarity of mind to be more productive in your work.

    Further, clutter does nothing but confuse your mind. It makes your area complicated and it shifts your focus from more important stuff to irrelevant items in your office. With your office free from clutter you will lessen distractions and allow Chi to flow more easily.

- **Meaningful career decorations**

    Putting Feng Shui decor in your office can help attract positive energy, especially decor which is meaningful to your career. For example, you could put in pictures and other inspirational items that represent success to motivate you to achieve your goals.

- **Have a natural air and light outlet**

    Air and light are very important in Feng Shui as these elements provide a great source of *Chi*. These are all the more needed in the workplace where stress and pressure can build up over time. Having good light and ventilation can help you and your workmates to get your fill of *Chi* as your day drains you out.

- **Put your desk in a commanding position**

    Attract strong success vibes in your workplace by placing your desk in a Feng Shui commanding position. To achieve this Feng Shui commanding position, your desk should be pointing towards the door and not behind it. It must also be far and not in line with the door. Note that it is also bad Feng Shui to place a desk facing a wall. If you have a small workplace where the 4 corners of the wall almost presses you in, try to make these walls disappear not physically but by the use of Feng Shui art, i.e. placing pictures in frames.

- **Take note of the North, South and Southeast area of your office**

    When it comes to the workplace, the most important areas are the North, South and Southeast areas of the Bagua. These directions represent fame, career path and prosperity.

    The North area represents career paths and is highly favored by the elements of water and metal. If you want your career path to be clear and good, it is advisable to put as much water and metal representation by putting in the colors blue and black (for water) and white (for metal). This can work wonder for people who are at a crossroads when it comes to their career choices. Strengthening the Feng Shui in this area will help you gain career perspective.

The South Area represents reputation and fame and is highly favored by the Feng Shui element of fire. To strengthen your reputation, it is advisable to put as much fire representation as possible in this area while avoiding water element representation such as fountains, aquariums and generally the color blue.

The Southeast area of your office represents wealth and abundance which is fed by the element of wood. As such, you would do well to put some wooden furniture and avoid items representing fire that could weaken the wood.

- **For home offices, place it as far away in your bedroom as possible**

   Having a home office can mix up your personal life and career, so it is always a favorite Feng Shui subject. The thin line that separates these two important aspects of life needs to be managed well or it will not work out.

   To further draw the line, make sure that you place your home office as far away from your bedroom as possible. If it can be done, have separate entries for these two rooms. This is because a different *Chi* is required for each room, one that calls for productivity and one that calls for relaxation.

Also, make it a point to not bring any of your personal items in your home office as this tends to blur the lines between your personal life and career. It will somehow confuse your mind though you may not be aware of it.

Apply these Feng Shui tips in your workplace now and see how the level of positive energy changes over time!

Chapter 4:
How to Get Rid Of Negative Vibes with Feng Shui

Conflicts are inevitable, but it doesn't mean you have to invite them in. More often than not, people don't see how negative *Chi* can cause conflicts to stir. The good news is that you are not totally helpless about it. You can actually minimize if not avoid these conflicts altogether by following these basic Feng Shui rules:

- **Eliminate Feng Shui problems in the main entry such as the following:**

    a) Mirrors facing the main door – Mirrors are often used in Feng Shui to deflect and re channel the energy around the house. If you put one in the main entry, it will push away all the energy that is about to enter your place. If you have a mirror facing the door, it would explain the lack of energy in your surroundings.

    b) Staircase facing the main door – Some Feng Shui experts would say that a staircase facing the door is bad Feng Shui because it rushes the *Chi* to either go up or go down, leaving the first level of your house more or less empty of *Chi*. Just to be sure, try to avoid building a staircase facing the door. If you must build a staircase, make it wide and curvy so that the *Chi* will flow through it and not just straight at it.

c) Walls too close to the main entry – Space is always an issue when it comes to Feng Shui. These spaces are marked or cut through by walls, so it is important that walls do not come too closely together or it will crowd the space. This is why walls should not face the main entry of the house too closely lest it blocks the space through which the *Chi* is absorbed.

d) Bathroom facing the main door – The bathroom is always associated with bad Feng Shui because it drains one of the most important Feng Shui elements – water. Though it does not hold true in all cases, the bathroom is still an exit point for the *Chi*. You wouldn't want it facing your main door because it might just go down the drain without first flowing through all the other areas of the house.

- **Conflicting Feng Shui elements in one place**

    As discussed in the previous chapters, Feng Shui is all about nature elements. Each element represents certain strengths and weaknesses. If placed in the right direction, these elements will do wonders in your life. However, conflicting elements if put together can weaken or even destroy an otherwise good Feng Shui.

    If your Feng Shui tells you to put some fire element in a certain area, do not defeat it by putting on some water elements too.

Below are the conflicting Feng Shui elements that you should not put together:

- Fire and Water

- Wood and Fire
- Earth and Water
- Metal and Water

Chapter 5:
Feng Shui for a Harmonious Life: Love & Marriage

Who wouldn't want a harmonious life filled with good relationships and prosperity? Feng Shui can definitely help you with that! Here are some Feng Shui tips for love, strong marriage and wealth!

Before you start with anything, you need to know that there is such a thing as a 'love corner' in every home's energy map (bagua). If you want your love/marriage to stay strong or improve, this is the area in your home that you should focus on. Once you determine where this 'love corner' in your home is located, you can start applying the Feng Shui tips below:

- The best colors for this love corner are red, pink and white. These colors symbolize love and passion in Feng Shui so it is always good to have them in your love corner.

- It is always best to put your bedroom in the love corner of your home. However, bedrooms are always considered as the love corner for the people in it, so don't forget to give it the same attention as you would in the love corner of your home.

- Avoid placing mirrors in your bedroom. Mirrors are active Feng Shui objects that will reflect any kind of energy (positive or negative) so it will create some kind of energy bouncing in the bedroom. Your bedroom should not be in the center of that. It should exude calm, passive energy.

- Keep your bedroom as bare and clutter-free as possible and avoid putting work papers, exercise machines, plants or even lots of pictures in there. These objects obstruct the passive flow of energy around the room.

- If you would have objects in the room, make sure that they're placed in pairs and there must not be a single object in there. For example, if you'd like to place a chair, put in two chairs instead of one chair only. This goes for single people who want to attract relationships too.

Follow these Feng Shui love tips and see your relationship strengthen from day to day!

Chapter 6:
5 Feng Shui Tips to Remember For Good Health

As the saying goes, health is wealth! But having a totally healthy mind and body seems to be more and more of a challenge nowadays with increasing pollution and health hazards.

To help you manage these health hazards and at the same time attract positive health energies, here are some Feng Shui health tips you should always keep in mind:

- Have fresh and good quality air in your home through the use of Feng Shui plants such as Areca and Bamboo Palm, English Ivy and Peace Lily. Quality air is the primary health foundation in Feng Shui.

- Always have natural light. While artificial light will suffice indoors and during night time, it is always best to have your fill of natural light. Natural light contains powerful and positive energy that will help your body achieve its maximum health.

- Get rid of the clutter in your home and workplace. Note that clutter contains very low and static energy which can suck out even the most positive energy in the room. Over time, clutter will drain your energy and will make you feel less healthy at the same time.

- The east area of your bagua is particularly concerned with your health. Nourish this part of the house by putting in water and wood elements such as lush wood and plants or fountains and aquariums. If you don't have much space, you can just represent these elements with their colors such as blue and black for water and brown and green for wood.

- Each person has his or her energy level that can be spent throughout the day. The reason why people don't have the same energy levels as the day ends is because some people spend too much energy on irrelevant things. Choose to spend your *Chi* wisely and have healthy energy throughout your whole day!

Chapter 7:
Feng Shui Colors

Color is synonymous to motion. Look closely and you'll discover that each hue possesses its own rhythm. As a homeowner, you are linked to the colors of your home through a variety of overlapping energy fields. For this reason, Feng Shui colors are influential elements that can create a great deal of difference in the general atmosphere and energy of a particular room. By understanding the basic definitions of colors, you will have an idea of how to select hues that are most advantageous for each room in your home. Furthermore, this knowledge will assist you in utilizing colors which best correspond to particular areas in the Feng Shui Bagua.

Colors of Fire

Red

The color red represents the fire element. When used in a room, this color can provide you with high levels of energy. Reddish hues can create a stimulating effect to the beholder. For this reason, you might want to consider adding small touches of crimson or scarlet in your home office or workspace. That said, beware of using too much red as this color also has the power to instigate aggression.

Red represents both power and passion. Use it when you wish to attract love and romance into your life. One of the best places to use red in the home would be in the bedroom, and in bagua areas that are concerned with relationships and love. However, when decorating your boudoir, try leaning towards more subdued earthy reds like Marsala or brick red.

Red invites luxury as well. For this reason, consider using the color in bagua areas concerned with abundance and prosperity. Another important thing to note is that these fire hues have the power to assist in transformation. Bagua areas relating to fame and reputation work best with reddish hues. The best areas to use red in the home would be your living room, your kitchen, and your dining area.

Orange

Orange is a secondary color that symbolizes the fire element. Orange is fun and youthful. It also represents ambition. Unlike red, orange has a slightly less stirring effect on the beholder. It is regarded as a friendly hue which makes it highly recommended for interior spaces. You can effectively use orange in bagua areas concerned with fame and reputation, specifically in areas where you wish to attract unity and teamwork. This is due to the fact that orange is a blended color.

When used in the dining area, orange hues have a positive effect on one's appetite. It also helps to inspire conversation. Orange shades are a great choice for the bedroom. However, be sure to go for more subdued earthy orange tones like Harvest Gold.

Purple

In Feng Shui, purple signifies nobility. This spiritual color is said to be connected with planes of higher consciousness. The use of purple in the home is highly advised especially when you find yourself in a life situation in which you are about to take on a big responsibility. (like a new job, starting a family, etc.) For homeowners who wish to attract wealth into their homes, the use of purple hues in the abundance and prosperity areas of the bagua is encouraged. If you are looking for romance, you may use purple in the bedroom. However, be sure to opt for lighter shades like lavender.

Pink

Like red, pink is a fire color that you can use to attract love and romance into your life. You may use it in the bedchamber or in bagua areas that correspond to relationships and love.

Yellow

Yellow is a fire color primarily chosen for its brightening and uplifting effect. Yellow symbolizes light. You can use it effectively in bagua areas concerned with abundance and prosperity. To the beholder, the color yellow creates the positive effect of increased productivity and heightened mental concentration. Use this color if you want to improve your memory. Because of this, yellow is a recommended color for your study.

Another thing to note is that yellow represents connection. Hence, it is perfect for bagua areas relating to fame and reputation as well is in areas of the home where you wish to obtain harmony. Such areas may include the living room and the dining room. Yellow is also a good choice for the kitchen. That said, avoid the use of this color in the bedroom. You may choose to add small touches of yellow in your room but be careful because too much yellow in the bedchamber can reinforce jealousy between couples. Yellow has the power to aggravate existing fears. Even for single individuals, yellow shades in the boudoir can amplify feelings of insecurity. You are advised against using the color in the bathroom as well. Generally, the use of yellows should be avoided in home areas dedicated to rest and relaxation.

Colors of Earth

Light Yellow

Bright yellow is indeed a fire color. Light yellow, on the other hand, is considered as an earth hue. Though the use of intense yellows for the bed and the bath is ill-advised, pale yellow shades are allowed.

Brown

Brown is an earth color that many people use for its grounding effect. The color indicates simplicity but it also shows stability. For this reason, it is a practical color of choice for areas of the bagua connected with skills and knowledge. To keep yourself grounded, you may add touches of brown in your living room or in your bedroom. Brown also has a comforting effect to the beholder.

Colors of Water

Blue

In Feng Shui, it is believed that blue is a symbol of honesty and steadfastness. Even without this knowledge, homeowners tend to choose this color due to its relaxing effect. Blue has the power to clear your mind as well as to promote learning. Thus, it is ideal for places in the home governed by the skills and knowledge area of the bagua.

For your bedroom, the incorporation of deep blue hues helps to promote sleep, and reduces stress and anxiety. Deep blue shades are also ideal for the bath.

Being the color of water, blue also symbolizes flow and creativity. Use this color in areas of the home in which you require inspiration. You may also utilize this color in bagua areas relating to abundance and prosperity.

Black

Like blue, this color of water also aids in maintaining serenity in your home. Use black in areas of the home where you need to obtain focus such as the skills and knowledge areas. Being a sophisticated color, hints of black are ideal for bagua areas relating to career and journey.

Colors of Wood

Green

Green is a wood color that symbolizes life and growth. Since greens can assist in healing, use this color if you wish to attract good health or experience speedy recovery from an ailment. More than that, greens like malachite, emerald, and jade are also effective in attracting good fortune into your home. If you wish to incorporate this color into your house, use them in bagua areas concerned with health. Use them as well in the family and elder's area of the Feng Shui bagua. Green is a sound option if you're contemplating about main colors for your living room or your family room.

Green is also ideal for bagua areas concerned with skills and knowledge due to the belief that it nurtures the mind and promotes mental balance.

Green yields a soothing effect, but more importantly, the color itself signifies cleansing. For this reason, greens are perfect for bathrooms.

Colors of Metal

White

The color white appeals to homeowners since it symbolizes purity and cleanliness. This is often the color of choice for bathrooms.

You should also know that white is a spiritual color that represents hope and goodness. Thus, the best places to use white would be the parts of the house governed by the creativity and children, helpful people and and travel areas of the bagua. Even so, you should not use white as the primary color of any room. This is because all-white rooms can diminish the flow of chi and this affects your ability to become open-minded.

Grey

Most homeowners select grey because it is conservative. However, you should avoid using it as a leading color for any room. Instead, use it as an accessory color to complement your primary color. Be warned that using too much grey can siphon your physical energy.

Follow this guide when choosing colors for the different rooms in your home, taking into consideration your primary intentions and the colors' effects to your physical, mental, and spiritual wellbeing. That said, you should also opt for colors which best reflect your personality and your goals in life. In the end, in arranging your home, you are advised to go with colors that inspire you and make you feel comfortable. For instance, pink can invite love and romance but if you or your partner is repulsed by the color, then it would be hard to count on its effectiveness.

Chapter 8: Bagua Map

The Bagua

The origins of the word bagua can be traced back to the sacred manuscript, I-Ching that translates to "The Book of Changes." The term bagua, traditionally epitomized as an octagon that consists of a center area and divided into eight sections, literally means "eight areas". These eight sections are referred to as trigrams.

Feng Shui practitioners use Baguas to define which areas of the home directly relate to particular areas of one's life. There are auspicious areas, meaning areas that consist of positive energy. Likewise, there are inauspicious areas that possess negative energy. It is necessary for you to note the auspicious areas so that you may find out how to enhance them. At the same time, being able to identify the inauspicious areas of your home will assist you in making use of Feng Shui cures which will invite and help the easy flow of positive chi throughout all areas of a particular living space and subsequently, to specific important areas of your life. When used correctly, the Feng Shui Bagua can lead the power of a homeowner's intention to their health, financial matters, intimate relationships, and more.

Life Areas of a Bagua

- Abundance and Prosperity
- Fame and Reputation
- Relationships and Love
- Family

- Health
- Creativity and Children
- Skills and Knowledge
- Helpful People and Travel
- Career and Business

What is a Bagua Map

For ease of use, particularly for the modern homeowner, the Feng Shui bagua's shape has been transformed from the traditional octagon to a square. The bagua square/ the bagua map is comprised of nine sections, all proportionate in size. Each of these segments is a gua area.

How to Use the Bagua Map

Abundance and Prosperity	Fame and Reputation	Relationships and Love
Family and Elders	Health	Children and Creativity
Skills and Knowledge	Career and Business	Helpful People and Travel

You can make your very own bagua map through the following steps:

- Obtain a piece of semi-transparent paper.
- Draw a perfect square on it.
- Divide the square equally into nine segments/ small squares.
- Label the sections appropriately with the different life areas:
- Southeast: Abundance and Prosperity
- South: Fame and Reputation
- Southwest: Relationships and Love
- East: Family and Elders
- Center: Health and Wellbeing
- West: Creativity and Children
- Northeast: Skills and Knowledge
- North: Career and Business
- Northwest: Helpful People and Travel
- Then, place the semi-transparent bagua map on top of the layout of your home. The bagua should divide your home space into nine different sections parallel to different life areas.

- Practitioners usually use the front door as a reference point. The North sector of your bagua map should fall directly above the front side of your home plan. Consequently, the bagua map's South sector should be situated on top of the layout. It's possible for your main door to fall in the North or Northeast or Northwest sectors. To determine proper placement of the bagua, ensure that your main door is located in any of the following gua areas:

- Skills and Knowledge

- Career and Business

- Helpful People and Travel

- If you own a large home, one energy center may end up spanning several rooms. On the other hand, if you live in a small space, one room may be governed by multiple energy centers. If you live in a house with more than one floor, make it your priority to map out the bagua on the ground floor. This space is the most significant since it contains the highest level of energy due to the constant activity pouring in from the main door. For individuals living in an apartment building, be sure to place the bagua map over the entrance of your apartment as opposed to the entrance of the building.

- Lastly, improve the different areas of your life (ex. marriage, money, health, etc.) according to Feng Shui practices. But of course, before doing that, you need to be familiar with each segment of the bagua and how each sector relates to the area(s) in your living space.

The Bagua Map Sectors

Each of the eight palaces (segments) of the bagua map are parallel to eight compass directions. They are also referred to as "the eight aspirations." The center of the bagua map is considered as the ninth sector.

The South Square (Fame and Reputation)

According to ancient Chinese belief, the South is considered as the most propitious direction. Thus, the South Square is situated at the top and is placed over your home plan as such. The element which governs the South Square is fire. Activate the fire element in the South sector of your home by decorating the rooms with fire colors such as red, orange, or pink. Furnish this area with floor lamps, table lamps, or candles and if possible, install a fireplace. As a result, you will experience more recognition which may be evident through career promotions or popularity in social groups.

Another thing that you can do to increase your luck in this area of your life is to hang your awards, degrees, or proof of any achievements in this area of your home. Other good enhancements would be triangular or pyramidal furniture, items made from leather, animal prints, and depictions of animals (animal paintings, wildlife photography, etc.)

You may also be interested in knowing that you can activate secondary elements to increase luck in each sector. For instance, wood feeds fire. And thus, using the wood element in the South (wooden furniture, etc.) can help invite more fame into your life. The lucky number for the South sector is 9.

The Southwest Square (Relationships and Love)

The earth element governs this "palace". Thus, if you wish to attract romance into your life or to improve an existing relationship, you need to incorporate earth elements into the Southwest sector of your home.

Activate the southwest sector of your home with the use of natural crystals such as rose quartz or amethysts. You may also furnish the room with clay pottery or ceramics. Mandarin ducks, due to their loyal and monogamous characteristics, are an Asian symbol of good marriage. For rooms occupied by husband and wife, a pair or ceramic Mandarin ducks (as well as other items that come in pairs) are a great idea. The same goes with the Double Happiness traditional Chinese ornament design on vases, rice bowls, or tea ware. Another thing that you can add to help strengthen relationship ties are photographs of loved ones or for married couples, some wedding pictures. Incorporate the color pink or red and some square shapes into the room.

Note that this sector does not just govern romantic relationships but also your ability to love and nurture yourself. The lucky number for the Southwest sector is 2.

The West Square (Creativity and Children)

This palace is linked to your descendant's good fortune. Thus, if your children are currently experiencing tough challenges, you may be able to help them by enhancing this sector. Improve this sector too if you're suffering from creativity blocks.

The soft metal element governs this region, metal furniture and art objects are advised for the room. If you plan to hang pictures of your children on the wall, consider using metal frames. Lucky colors for this sector include white, silver, gold, copper, and brass. 7 is a lucky number for this area. You may place seven metal coins in this zone for good luck when it comes to giving birth, whether it's to kids or to brilliant ideas. Rounded or oval items signify completion so be sure to incorporate them into this space as well.

The Northwest Square (Helpful People and Travel)

This palace governs your luck when it comes to finding mentors or people who will help you in developing new skills or gaining knowledge. The nature element connected with this sector is hard metal. Thus, you need to decorate the corresponding room with metal objects. A great suggestion is a six-rod wind chime; you may also use crystals. Decorate the room with metal colors like gold, grey, and silver. Another thing that you can do to activate this sector is by adding a book or an artwork created by a famous expert in your field. You may also place a portrait of an influential person who has inspired you or made a great difference in your life. Note also that this area doesn't just govern help from the seen realms but from the unseen realms as well. To invite guidance and help from beneficial people or spirits, place a crystal bowl in this space. If you wish to be able to travel more often, add maps, globes, travel brochures, travel logs, or travel magazines in this sector. Number 6 is the lucky number for the Northwest sector.

The North Square (Career and Business)

The North sector influences your success when it comes to your career and source of livelihood. If this area in your life could use an extra boost, be sure to activate this palace. The North is connected to water and so it is a good place to install fountains or an aquarium. However, to invite good luck, you need to ensure that the water flows into the room as opposed to flowing out of it. If placing a fountain indoors is not an option for you, then make use of glass or mirrors instead.

It would also be beneficial to know that metal feeds water. Hence, adding metal objects into the room may also help in improving one's career and business opportunities. Use water colors for this room such as deep blues or black. Decorate the area with wavy shapes and sinuous textiles. Keep in mind that the lucky number for the North sector is 1.

Be aware that the North palace does not only affect your career but also your general path in life.

The Northeast Square (Skills and Knowledge)

This sector is concerned with education. This is not just restricted to academics but also includes career training and independent studies. If you need to study for an examination, then activating the Northeast palace will bring you great advantage. This region is linked to the earth element and so you may activate it with the use of crystals, bright lighting, or pottery.

Another thing that you can do is to incorporate symbols of education such as books. The Northeast sector is an excellent place to build a study area. If you plan to place artwork in the room, make sure that it depicts a scene of stillness or contemplation. Decorate the room with green hues or dark blues and consider using square furniture. The lucky number for this area is 8.

Note that more than just governing your knowledge and skills, this sector also represents your spiritual and inner growth.

The East Square (Family and Elders)

This palace represents your ancestors. It also symbolizes growth and vitality. The wood element governs this sector. Thus, it would be wise for you to decorate the corresponding room with plants. If this is not a possibility, try making use of botanical prints or green décor. Also make it a point to include furniture that's made of wood or made to resemble wood. The recommended color is green. Make use of tall vertical furnishings such as columns and floor lamps. You may also add family photos unless the east square falls over a bedroom. The lucky number for this area is 3.

It is also good to know that this sector does not just govern your family life but also influences your ability to create new beginnings.

The Southeast Square (Abundance and Prosperity)

This is the palace which controls your luck when it comes to wealth and prosperity. The element associated with the Southeast sector is wood, though the best lucky color is said to be purple. Green, gold, red, and blue are money colors which invite the flow of cash.

If your intention is to earn a larger income for yourself or for the entire family, activate this area with the use of plants. Remember that water feeds wood and so adding water features may enhance the effect.

Decorate this room with objects that symbolize wealth to you such as gold ingots, coins, or wealth ships. Alternatively, you can include images of things or accomplishments that you are grateful for. Rectangular shapes are recommended when selecting furniture. The lucky number for the Southeast sector is 4.

The Center Square (Health)

Some Feng Shui practitioners are so concerned with obtaining abundance and prosperity or love and relationships that sometimes, they tend to neglect this very essential sector. It is important to realize that without good health, everything else that you possess or have accomplished will eventually fall apart. More than influencing health, the Center palace also governs growth and longevity. This area is associated with the earth element and thus you may decorate it with earthenware. Excellent color choices include green, brown and earthy yellows.

In choosing plants for this room, make sure that you go for the ones with round or oval leaves. Bear in mind that plants with pointed leaves can pose a threat to your wellbeing as they form poison arrows.

The center square is also the area of balance. Consider hanging a yin yang image or any symbol that represents balance. The lucky number for this area is 5.

Chapter 9:
Feng Shui Origins and History

Some practitioners believe that Feng Shui dates back 2,000 years ago, originating in the mountains of Southwest China. There are also those who believe that Feng Shui may be traced back to 6,000 years ago, existing long before our predecessors even learned the art of writing. Feng Shui was used in Ancient China in order to secure the power, the wealth, and the health of the ruling dynasties. Feng Shui practitioners of that time found themselves rising into respectable places in the society. The masters have passed the knowledge of Feng Shui down to their disciples and from generation to generation through a discriminating process.

The Han Dynasty (206 BC to 220 AD)

The earliest records related to the practice of Feng Shui can be traced back to this era. Practitioners back then used the science and art of Feng Shui to determine the auspicious areas for building homes, villages, and even burial sites. In the succeeding centuries, Feng Shui practitioners continuously practiced and developed, leading to the creation of the Form School in the Tang Dynasty.

The Tang Dynasty (618 to 906 AD)

During this time, the existing philosophies of Feng Shui came together in what is known as the Landscape School. As the name suggests, its primary purpose is to determine which areas in the landscape possess good chi. This is done for the protection of the people. The practice of Feng Shui at this time placed great emphasis on mountains, valleys, hills, bodies of water, and other features of the landscape. They also emphasized the importance of erecting buildings that are in harmony with the universe. According to the Form School of Feng Shui, even the smallest things such as a tiny pebble possesses life and chi. Thus, it has the power to either energize you or to destroy you.

In 888 AD, Master Yang Yun Sung developed the Compass School of Feng Shui. He stressed the importance of choosing a site that possesses the dragon's energy. Sites with rocks in the shape of the dragon, the turtle, or birds were believed to be lucky. At this point, the practice of Feng Shui had grown to become more refined. Later, his teachings and writings became great classic sources in the study of Feng Shui and its history.

The Song Dynasty (960 AD to 1279)

By this time Master Wang Chih had refined Yang Yun Sung's practices. In fact, much of the knowledge in the contemporary Compass School of Feng Shui is based on Wanh Chih's principles. Compared to the Form School of Feng Shui, the the Compass School follows a more scientific approach involving the use of the compass, numerology, mathematics, as well as the I-Ching and the bagua which were used to analyze the energy of a given area. Among the most well-known theories employed in this school are:

- the yin-yang
- the five elements
- the Lo-Shu Square

The late 19th century saw the merging of these two separate schools.

Ming Dynasty (1368 to 1644) – Quing Dynasty (1644 to 1912)- Chinese Cultural Revolution (1966 to 1976)

Feng Shui continued to be widely practiced throughout the Ming and the Quing dynasties. But after the fall of the Quing dynasty, its practice was discouraged by the Chinese government and by the Communist government in 1946. In the advent of the Cultural Revolution, many texts about Feng Shui were destroyed. Feng Shui practitioners were forced to flee the country, seeking sanctuary in countries with Chinese communities, from Singapore to San Francisco. This was how Feng Shui ultimately found its way into the West where it continued to thrive as westerners began discovering the value of chi and Feng Shui practice.

Feng Shui Today

Nowadays, Feng Shui is once again popularly observed in China. Modern Feng Shui often utilizes a combination of the two traditional schools of Feng Shui, giving rise to different variations of this practice including Symbolic Feng Shui. Examples of popular Chinese Feng Shui symbols are:

- Peony Flowers and The Dragon and the Phoenix for love and marriage

- Chinese Coins, the Three Legged Toad and the Crystal Tree for wealth

- Fu Dogs, the Golden Cicada, the Mystic Knot, and the Horse for protection and good fortune

- The Buddha, the Wu-Lou Gourd, the Lucky Bamboo, and the Butterfly for happiness, health and longevity

Chapter 10:
The Use of Nature in Your Home With Feng Shui

The Lucky Bamboo

Add green plants into your living space. This may include cuttings from your yard. It not only invites energy but it also filters the air in the room. The Lucky Bamboo is perhaps one of the best known Feng Shui cures as it is believed to attract not only wealth but love and happiness as well. The bamboo is the ultimate symbol of strength, wisdom, and flexibility and thus, it has the power to free your spirit and heal your being.

Your lucky bamboo plant should symbolize the unity of all five elements. The bamboo itself symbolizes wood, and the rocks that it grows in signify the earth element. Water your plant regularly to fortify the water element. To add in the fire element, tie a red ribbon around the plant. Incorporate the metal element by making use of a glass pot or if you prefer using ceramic pots for your plants, include a metal coin or a metallic Laughing Buddha figurine. Grow your lucky bamboo stalks in the health, wealth, or family areas of the bagua.

How many bamboo stalks should you have? It depends on your intention. You'll need nine bamboo stalks if you wish to invite good fortune. You'll need eight if you wish to obtain wealth. If health is your goal, then opt for five. Grow three for happiness, and for love and marriage, two bamboo stalks should do just fine.

Flowers

If it's not possible for you to add plants, try picking fresh flowers weekly. However, you must change the water daily and dispose of the flowers as soon as you observe signs of wilting. Note that dying flowers tend to create a negative effect by attracting undesirable energy. Popular flowers for Feng Shui include the lotus for purity and cherry blossoms for marriage, health, and new beginnings. If you wish to achieve balance in life or to have a smooth-sailing life, opt for chrysanthemums. The narcissus flower is a good choice if you wish to further your career.

Aquariums

Fishes that are associated with wealth and prosperity include the arowana, the goldfish, and koi. How many fish should you have? Consider having eight red fish and one black. The purpose of the black fish is to repel the negative energy. It is necessary to maintain the cleanliness of the aquarium and should any of the fish die, be sure to replace it immediately.

To avoid inviting negative energies into your home, refrain from keeping aquariums in the kitchen or in the bedroom. Instead, place your aquarium in the wealth or career areas of the bagua. If you wish to install the aquarium in your wealth area, a square-shaped fish tank is recommended. However, if you prefer a round shape, opt for small fish bowls to prevent the metal element from overpowering the wood element.

Fountains

As previously mentioned, when installing indoor fountains, the water should flow inwards not outwards. However, not all living spaces will permit the installation of wall-mounted water fountains. If such is the case, consider a small fountain for your tabletop. If this still isn't possible, portraits or photographs of flowing water are also acceptable.

Water fountains invite wealth and prosperity. They are best placed in the East, the Southeast, and the North. Refrain from placing fountains in the South area because this will drown out the fire element that it needs. Furthermore, avoid installing fountains in the bedroom because they will invite sorrow and anxiety. You may add crystals and stones to strengthen the good energy.

Fruits

Fruits provide the home with the energy of fruition. If it's not possible for you to keep fresh fruits in the house, consider hanging paintings or artistic photographs of fruits. Feng Shui practitioners refer to peaches as the Fruit of Heaven, because they are connected with wealth and health as well as with love and marital success. Grapes are a symbol of abundance. They are also known to be an infertility cure. Use apples if you wish to obtain peace and harmony under your roof. Red apples are considered to be extremely lucky. Pineapples herald good luck and they symbolize wealth and prosperity.

Conclusion

Thank you again for downloading this book!

I hope this book was able to help you learn more about feng shui!

The next step is to put this information to use, and begin using feng shui in your home!

Finally, if you enjoyed this book, please take the time to share your thoughts and post a review on Amazon. It'd be greatly appreciated!

Thank you and good luck!

www.ingramcontent.com/pod-product-compliance
Lightning Source LLC
LaVergne TN
LVHW021740060526
838200LV00052B/3387